Inner Voice spea
inspiring, and
top quality colle
uine melange of intellectual depth with unpretentious beauty, will find its way to public libraries and private bookshelves in various countries… A remarkable literary event…

—Daniela Culen, MA Librarian, Canadian National Library and Archives, Ottawa

This work uniquely responds to the covert needs of human psyche in turbulent times… The written by a psychologist-poet masterful must-read for anyone, who formulates questions about one's own place and direction within the overwhelming complexity of our rapidly changing world…

—Duncan Scott MD Psychiatrist, Queens University, Kingston

Having experienced the close range combat has caused my encounter with the long range ideas in this very special book even more enlightening… These pages got destined to engage and inspire those fortunate enough to discover them…

—G.J. Hutchinson, Infantryman, Canadian Armed Forces

This author has the rare gift of taking ordinary words, and transforming them into spirit-laden lyrics. As with the works of other outstanding poets, a great role is played by the metaphor, and emotions in the exploration of life with all of its fables, drama, and tragedy. This is an exquisite cornucopia of accessible life stories that could only be written by one who had lived them without compromise.

—Barbara Nixon, Partner, Promeus Inc. Toronto

INNER VOICE

INNER VOICE

Witold Poplawski

Tate Publishing & *Enterprises*

This title is also available as a Tate Out Loud product. Visit www.tatepublishing.com for more information.

Published by Tate Publishing & Enterprises, LLC
127 E. Trade Center Terrace | Mustang, Oklahoma 73064 USA
1.888.361.9473 | www.tatepublishing.com

Tate Publishing is committed to excellence in the publishing industry. The company reflects the philosophy established by the founders, based on Psalm 68:11,
"The Lord gave the word and great was the company of those who published it."

Cover & Interior Design by Leah LeFlore
Illustrations by Tomasz Poplawski

Published in the United States of America

ISBN: 978-1-60604-975-4
1. Poetry/Inspirational & Religious
08.10.09

DEDICATION

In memory of Urszula Poplawski.
Dedicated to my Family and its Canadian extension—employees of Ontario Corrections.

ACKNOWLEDGMENT

I wish to thank Tom Poplawski and Wayne Moore for their valuable suggestions. Also my special thank-you to Tom Poplawski for his creative illustrations.

TABLE OF CONTENTS

FOREWORD

It is not uncommon for us to have times or seasons in life when we find that our deep and unarticulated feelings are searching for a voice with which to speak to others and ourselves. During such special times, some of us might choose to hide in "numbing bottles" of different shapes and sizes. Others seek out those who may hold up helpful lenses, through which we can examine the pervasive unknown in ourselves and in the world around us. All too often in this competitive world, many rush at us with their single lens of choice and unending superlatives, too much protesting that we need not look anywhere else.

However, those fortunate enough to have this open-minded, spiritually, intellectually, also artistically mature book in hand will be in company of a truly unique person, and profound yet accessible poet. Herein Dr. W. Poplawski nudges us to look at the human experience through the equally valid lenses of spirituality, philosophy, and psychology. Doing so, he proves that the superb food for thought can be lively interesting, emotionally compelling, and make an excellent, unforgettable read.

His outstanding work is liberally sprinkled with references from classic literature, history, and reflects with insight the human condition as seen by an experienced psychologist on the same journey. As with all lucidly sophisticated yet reader-friendly, thus comparatively rare poetry, this creative collection invites, even compels us to pause... Also, it gently assists us in revisiting personal sacred spaces and places, with the aim of providing our souls with a chance to catch up to our hurried bodies.

We have been given this highly reflective, quietly inspiring, often surprisingly beautiful collection of poems from someone who has respect for the Divine, faith, and the real wealth of multifaceted practical experiences from the life journey of a common soul. The well from which this clear water has been drawn can be glimpsed by pausing over the autobiographical text entitled "The Gift."

—Rev. Wayne B. Moore

AUTHOR'S NOTE AND ACKNOWLEDGMENT

Once, I used to make a living with my hands among other factory workers and coal miners. Then I worked with my mind, whether at the vibrant universities or frozen in time prisons. In all the above working environments, I've had the privilege to meet my unassuming teachers. Luckily, they came from diverse educational levels, ethnicities, races, and religions. Without them sharing their feelings, thoughts, and silent presence, there wouldn't have been a chance for me to now share, via the written words' instrument, my thoughts on the elusive theme: the mysterious sense of life. They all deserve my grateful acknowledgement. The acknowledgement below requires some explanation though.

Having published a few works in Polish before, I settled down in Canada. Then I became deterred by the seemingly insurmountable challenge of viable literary expression in a second language. Unlike Jozef Korzeniowski, who left his narrow street, one close to mine, in the old city of Cracow to become the Victorian era's illustrious English writer Joseph Conrad, I didn't believe in my ability to create any literary works in English. For over twenty years I remained artistically mute, fortunately never blind and deaf. For example, clarity-poetry and graphics of the Canadian Aboriginal artist Michael Robinson have made an inspiring impression on me.

One day I came across the on-line essay by the Newsweek columnist, Rabbi Marc Gellman. I've tended to follow his texts, after reading his eulogy on the passage of John Paul II. As a psychologist, once close to some in his intellectual circle in Cracow, I felt intrigued by the accuracy with which the author defined the late Pontiff's personality. Interestingly, that best eulogy came from the sphere of Judaism in the homogenous body of human spirituality. This new short essay has influenced my life via advice I call the "Gellman's Equation." In brief, his "e=mc2" of applied spirituality went as follows:

Only the lucky few are blessed with an opportunity, of gainfully doing what they genuinely would like to do until the end of their productive years. The others ought to seriously ask themselves, what contribution they would *really* enjoy to give in the remaining part of their lives, had they a choice. The self-answer will come, as we all have been given a degree of very different gifts. After finding and utilizing one's own gift, the rewarding enjoyment follows. One may be quite good at that particular activity. If not making a living from it, one still ought to find the way of doing it in one's spare time. Otherwise, one wouldn't self-realize and never discover one's own true potential.

I did ask myself the above question. The answer came. I ought to continue with my passion-hobby of stonemasonry and, very much so, to write poetry and the short forms of prose... in English. Again, I felt inhibited. That same day, despite obstacles, I'd resolved that if Rabbi Gellman had been right, there must be a way. I should show trust, ask for the silent guidance, and start writing. It has worked. The lines of "Inner Voice" began emerging... I wish to acknowledge the hand that electronically passed me a key for the unlocking of the long confined, if readying potential. I'll be honoured if this little book could modestly assist in the awakening of any dormant positive potential in my reader.

THE FORCE

for Anna Hutchinson

The force of love is serpent-apt yet flint-like invincible
In shrewd disguise of naïve helplessness

It still may, before time's blank horizon arrives
Patiently–drop by drop–reduce the world's painful fear
Petrified into the aging logic of wars

Its bright younger sibling–wisdom in life
Requires the daily gift of bread and wine from selfless love
For own precious fragile existence

Without love's caring touch, it would slowly shrink back
To the former thin empty shell of mere intelligence

Once left alone–hungry and thirsty intelligence
In despair translates the hurting fear to stiff illogic of hate
For love–to reveal it's coiled force

SOME TRUTH ABOUT POETRY

Poetry somewhat resembles a stern surgical art
probing the covert inner sense
in the carefully re-analyzed
tangible body of the overt one
with the self-commissioned task
of dissecting these invisible findings
into the–hopefully available–
shades of their meanings

It is, contrary to lofty myths,
a stonemason's dry craft of cutting
with the frequently sharpened mental chisel
through the resistant interiors
of dug-out, by the strained mind,
imaginary granite fieldstones
in order to finally split them
exactly the precise way
one thinks and feels they will fit

A poet possibly acts as a quasi-sorcerer
attempting to animate
the life deprived objects of own choice
revelling in time and space
even if hopelessly blindfolded
And trying to cast that subtle spell
on the unsuspecting topics
regardless how challenging lyrically
or enforcing the acceptance of rejection
they may prove to be

A tapped by poetry, scout of the Far Abstract

Theory surgeon–patient word-mason
Misinterpreted paper wizard
Rookie prospector of Near Beyond
after years of work in self doubt
might non-intrusively submit
the panned out, in the upstream of reality,
few miniscule nuggets
to the less than limited attention
of the sympathetic good merchants
busy down the river

THE SCULPTURE

Once at early dawn born
This time-resistant marble
It must have waited endlessly
To then become shaped
By the long forgotten hands
Into an epitome of beauty
One fleetingly reflected
Within this grand museum
By passing generations
Of the equally forgotten
Innumerable pairs of eyes

THE WINGS OF EARTH

for Aleksandra Nesovic

What else these living rocks are
Other
Than the hard patiently busy Earth's palms
Covered with the creation friendly
Sun fertilized dust?

They anew hold us gently tight
Like meek hatchlings
Before re-launching the old-new birds
Having rehearsed how to fly
On their barely fledgling wings

We all return here–far beyond often
To strengthen our feeble wings
Warm them with little sparks of joy
Yet they grow ever painfully
Coral reef-slowly

Then–from clarity's peak
Where they can stretch wide enough
To quest for a love equally selfless
As fearless
We soar to incredible heights
Or–exhilarated drops of nostalgia
Dissolve in the heart of Light

STONEHENGE

The nearly lost
Universal symbol
Of the inner sanctum
Unfolds in a circle
As naturally
As the same sun
Remains the first
Of all visible objects
To worship

The silence of stone
Has always been
An excellent conductor
Of ancient truth
That is why
The hidden sense
Encircled by huge rocks
Recaptures us
From within

THIS MYSTERY

As virtually everything
that in a miracle flows from the unseen
Also this mystery
strives to manifest here
but possibly because
of its infinitely delicate spirit
remains discerning
beyond comparison

This mildly misanthropic mystery
appears preferring
to modestly enter our world
through the back door of wild nature
and seems somehow partial
towards flowers birds
mountain ranges
clouds or dolphins' dance

For some reason
presumably well known to itself
this mystery tends–albeit tactfully–
to avoid most humans
yet doesn't reach the point
of complete exclusion
One unsustainable
Under natural universal laws

So–it accordingly dwells
in the subtle dreams of chosen children
until they grow up
And if it genuinely has enjoyed
that experience
It would leave a gift behind
One deposited with great care
In their eyes' smiles
or the future luminescent products
of their unexplainably
phototropic minds

MINIATURES I

Spring

From the dried shelter
of the shell opened on time
emerges–if hesitantly
awe fresh–so much surprised…

Flowerbeds

Through play of shades, time narrows space
in which die down flowers' mute circles
Thoughts under surface of all things plain
follow slow current in silence's realm

Winter Comes

The leafless frost tree–yearning home
extends its branches smooth silver-toned
towards the ice-etched doors glassy-cold
New season reigns from clouded heights
Window-glued children start their flight
to catch soft feathers–of the doves white…

NORTHERN SUN

for Jerzy Bahr

A caribou ghost's skull
turning to stone
A grounded small boat
braves against seasons
among the wind-dried waves of grasslands

Its non-existing ears
follow faint sounds of steps long gone
Nostrils' hollowness
sips vanished scents from pallid rivers

The birch-bark far northern sun
grudgingly recovers
Brought back to its life
by a pious wolf's fiercest night prayers

THE REFLECTION

for Father Horst Seidel

Has not the first reason for all that exists
been true longing to become perceived
Felt by the objectless, yet in love, Awareness?
Perhaps that might suggest as to why
it seems to be gently sending subtle signals
or playwriting magnificent spectacles
reminding us about its cryptic lone existence
Us–the dispensed into forming matter
wild fire-winds scattered–seeds of Itself
Now re-connecting to evolve in awe
a live mirror–reflecting that primal love–
Focused by the sentient Aim-bound entities
feeling its vibration through their senses…

RILKE'S POETRY

Not only the Emperor's sun-wheeled chariot
perpetually evolving itself
rolls on–all comprised of eternity
It is also invincibly cloaked

The born to fight yet heeding gladiator
in the dust covered arena
has a thin shield of his fifty years only
but holds a brazen spear
The far extending masterful mind

This formidably sharp spear
had penetrated already
the hidden interior of the surrounding world
to open it–for aiming higher

How could it have ever happened
that this hopelessly brief and non-Homeric
one-sided quasi duel
has cut to the very essence of beauty
merely composing true words?

INNER VOICE

The human inner voice
wild nature's most unique part
inconsistently enough
sadly unprotected
under any bylaw regulations
often forced to starvation
through all seasons hunted
disappears not unlike
white bears threatened
with extinction

The organized all-audacious
cacophony of the outer sounds
tries hard to shrink
if possible pin down
then convert it to a dusty item
to be hidden in the museum
of human curiosa
or enrich the retro-Barnum circus
beside its iconic
lady bearded well

Every yet unregulated host
of the inner voice
(Freelance protecting
its questioned existence)
is naturally reciprocated though
by this grateful fugitive
with the ultimate
life's time stewardship
through the offered free of charge
very best advice

If genuinely asked to assist
it will lucidly tell one what to pursue
and even what way
and afterwards realistically explain
what to avoid
also–when and how
the challenge is
that the inner voice
just delicately whispers
while the global cacophony
plays frantically loud

MINIATURES II

Either Or

Bewildered–he knows not
if life is caused
by a self-governing chemistry
or the ageless Phoenix
that hatched the round universe
laying an egg?

Quest

In the quest endless
Wearing out sandals
Sat down to discover
The horizon is–here

Five Senses

The force concealed
removes its light from an amber
above the sea's edge
Poverty with five senses
in a shy attempt came here
to talk to God…

THE MEDITATION ROOM

Pure and simple–though elusive wisdom–
sampling with panache modest tiny things
finds all natural to twice daily focus
on the crisp-bitter taste in finest green tea

For a long time adored and pursued beauty
does never forget to re-contemplate
these addictively regular blue patterns
on the old tea bowl in the best of white shade

Why then harmony–thoughtfully invited–
accepts short visits in a well prepared cell
of this, to life's wheel sentenced spiritual being
Before–with vague smile–excuses itself?

Z E N M A S T E R

For the clarity
Fully freed
From the hypnotic
Non-essential
Such suffices:
Meditation
Working with hands
Helping students
A roof above the head
Of straw mat
An old kimono
Buddha's tiny statue
Handful of rice
A bowl of tea
The last haiku
After that–
Sheer Void

"There can be a young head on the old neck
and an old head on the young one"
—Dhammapada

THE YOGA WAY

for Tananda Yogi

Do you feel sorry for that skeleton
with eyes–distant flames–
Left on dust-wind but by a miracle
sitting ramrod-straight?

No need noticing me–a wrench
sunken in grinding poverty
Hiding inside the cave of madness
plotting my own pitiful death…

My dear little brother I do not see
your body–looking inward–
But do love you–a transient shiny
particle in all that exists

Everything unfolds as relative
in this world of appearances
Why would our souls' so diversified age
–be any different?

I've trained long to finally accelerate
my true inner growth–
Became older than you and departed
the point in time we shared…

I did pass the path that slowly leads
mankind from childish fears
To adolescent warlike assertions
to mature adult cooperation

Now I grow very old–into the last phase
of loving all that is
So do naturally refocus my only affect
on the one Source behind

Do you cherish your fierce reward
life awards for procreation?
I brush with the ultimate prize
the hidden gate pays for no-return…

CHRISTIAN MYSTIC

He had smelted his searching mind to red-hot
in faith having found the lost intuition-compass' needle
long covered by the overgrown forest
of mundane childlike logic

Now prays with the skull lowered and closed eyes
before leaving the subsiding sounds of his former world
as the sapphire flame unbounded up flows
burning all of no substance

THE VERSES FROM SHIRAZ

for Helen Yazdani

Even an innately sophisticated
nobly educated poet
while self-absorbed lyrically
with one soul-mate's love
does face a risk
of becoming a fine poetry's potter
who–masterly, subtly–
spins the clay-less wheel...

Then–how a humble worker
veiled by a far language
addressing his love
in straightforward verses
could stunningly win his case
in as focused as the Holy Inquisition
the histories of literature
- Immortal court?

There is no satisfying answer
If there is any at all
to the above, too good a question
Unless–one could
from the time-vehicle–
ask in old Farsi one smiling Hafiz
why he intimately adores
the ever-present to him
God
Whom–he–met
Under the name of
Allah

THE CHURCH

By the roughest edges of life hurt
a young man has resolved to firmly seek God
thus–long and hard he thought
Then he projected the ideal if imaginary church
set within his mind's walls
The impressive temple of not a dissimilar kind
to the one his mother used to take him to
when he was a little boy

As he continued failing in his quest for God there
much disheartened, he soon forgot
the first abstract creation
and erected a profoundly esoteric chapel instead
marked with in-depth spiritual symbols
from across faith's ages
of the greatest cathedrals, synagogues, mosques
Far Eastern shrines, pagan altars
he had ever seen, heard of, or conceived
Alas he did not meet the elusive Aim even there
so grieving the dead meaning–of his life
He climbed the highest of cliffs at night
but on the open edge halted
before catching the much swifter wings of wind
He glanced at the radiantly stellar ocean above
for his utterly last time
and all of a sudden did sense the sign
from the Force Undefined he had been looking for
all along the winding way

Since the glimpse of The Face smiling behind life
until he passed–an aged man

Due to his gratefulness and loyalty he often felt like
silently praying and meditating
in the same small church
his young mother cared to take him as a child to
But in an unrecorded miracle
the modest temple has changed its timid shape
hosting the shore-less ocean
encrusted with the golden islands
of busy suns–feeding their hungry planets
- The warm breathing universe

A nobly fragrant rose confessed
- I salute beauty almost every day
when the shield of fire submerges
and those mystery birds of dusk
chase the copper droplets falling
from the slowly melting skies
- I greet beauty by responding
with acceptance to all final events
and with focus–to all plain things
conveyed a wayside hawthorn

ONE SHINY LAKE IN ONTARIO

Unlike an overly timid pond
my lake displays itself as assertive
albeit without
those carried away mood swings
of a too independent sea

It modestly contains at bay
all its due sunsets following sunrises
Yet within the pretty reasonable
frame of reference

Sure it doesn't aim to reach the horizon
instilling concerns
what might be brewing behind its thin
un-tangible border

Even a lure ambushing sleepy bass
wouldn't create a tidal wave
Remaining mindful
where the fine line is

Clearly no loon scanning these waters
would ever become lost
in between the quite workable elements
of foam and wind

Under calmer conditions
my lake writes, paints, plays old violin
or slowly sculpts the canoeing clouds
in its own silent image

THE PETROGLYPHS BY STONEY LAKE

for Michael Robinson

With no finesse of limestone arches
No altar stunning the breath away
No music notes transformed to light
that flows via the colourful laceworks
of glass mosaics conceived by art
It feels like finding the lost surprise
Ghost Notre Dame–out in the wild

As though foreseeing the childlike us
Kind native spirits from muted past
through anonymous sentient old hands
have offered us–what they felt best
The artful beacon of rock-carved shapes
In vast cathedrals–we to see fail
Left on wind footprints–aiming at sky

THE OJIBWAY ISLAND

Any isle or an island proper
is a cast away part of its own past
A land-post once able
to have stopped the rising waters
exactly at where
they outlined physical perimeters
got destined to stay
Afterwards long resembling
a buoyant heavenly body
or a dry sponge
that soaks the cloaked vibrations
Gently awakening
the new sunrise enigma
of an ascent renewing life

Remaining all of the above–
The watching from the lake's bay
My life's early sunset
This sickle-shaped Horseshoe Isle
stretched barely enough
to support a name
boasts some rare additional assets–
is symmetrically cosy
like ducklings small fleets
Annually concocts
To the most pristine standards–
its poison-ivy brew
and quickly shape-shifts
to a hard lucky-horseshoe
on the threshold of frosty night

THE SMALL PENNISULA GARDEN

As no thinker ever defined a size of Eden
Even a small garden appropriate to means
might pass for a time circumvented paradise

Various innocent birds seem to assume so
they freely "sleep around" before nestling
and leisurely enjoy a birdbath fully naked

Unlike that fast crowd the more serious veggies
in noble stupor, do not care about pleasures
Instead focusing on slow personal growth

The puzzling world of the seductive flowers
appears to exist–somewhere in between
Bound yet responsive to the whims of wind

Own immortality pre-arranging chipmunks
harvest their tomatoes' ripe annual crops
storing in full cheeks what a busy life brings

An Antique Shop

A blue fish's fierce jump
as if through the ring of fire
defines an old teapot

Next–a plum tree paints
the foam of moonstruck petals
softer than white ash

In a Capsule Hotel

The ending at dawn
Sheltered in a beehive
All different dreams

The working culture
Never indulging itself
To briefly trespass

A Green Rice-Cake

The curved roof's shade
along an ancient passage
slows a passer by
Honouring the guests
a gracious aged lady's
pure silk kimono
The sweetened beans'
in a green chewy rice-wrap
frugally mild taste

The Monument

The fame–stone or bronze-friendly
won by some military leaders
and vision-pregnant politicians
also by the artists heavens' gifted
even by a few holiest irregulars
tends to morph–post mortem–
towards the imposing monuments
in all the cities affluent enough
Surprise–in the Taipei's center
the only monumental statue
enshrines the deeply buried in time
explorer of prudence: Confucius

A Small Teahouse

In the plainly adorned teahouse
perched on a jade-green slope
a clay teapot patiently brews
in a quiet unpretentious way
the healing bowls of oolong
for the two searching lives
re-connecting so-brief-so-fast

The Tower

Boldly challenging the sky
A glass-protected top
of the bamboo-stem shaped
Earth's highest tower
offers a good vantage point

for the quick scanning
of the city's vast outline
One eclipsed by steep hills
adjacent to zeroing slowly
the harsh offshore storm

FRANCE TRAVEL-NOTES

The White Seagulls

The supple all target-aimed seagulls
gliding above this stern
Normandy's beach
don't mourn the away passing names
"Omaha" or "Juno"
Just circle and circle
in their swooping pursuit of hard life

Yet these wind piercing sharp sounds
The old anthem of seagulls
Finely encrusted
into the Andre Rieu's harmony-music
"The Fallen Heroes"
helps one to hear
their "To-Whom-The-Bell-Tolling"
afar–in that gone war's cry…

The Mercury Temple's Ruins

In the Ouverne's heart–off beat
on the chilly in-clouds peak
of the very highest one
From the ages-inactive volcanoes
the Roman temple of Mercury
vaguely points both
to the past–and the future
via its deaf-mute stones
wrapped in the thickening wet fogs

CHILE TRAVEL-NOTES

The Inca Lake–El Portillo

Against its cloudless lapis-lazuli lid
the Andean-rustic goblet
of the sunlit rocks
unforgiving and steep
contains an icy cobalt-blue lake
on the bottom now distant

Awaiting by the foot-wide "camino"
a lone hairy-grey spider
clinging to a tiny bush
accented with some yellow flowers
tells a solitary trekker
to start carefully descending
Not looking down…

Pablo Neruda's House

Quite many of us adore women
or contemplate ocean
if tired with too verbose nightlife

Less–flirt with communism
while concurrently
living well in three fine houses

Much less - write the best poetry
and almost no one
wins the Nobel Prize for it
Yet only the deceased Pablo
in front of his house
received a small amphitheatre

Now the couples in fresh love
come to gaze silently
at the door *he* used to open

THE ANCIENT SHORES

for Petro Koukidis

Sage Heraclit's "panta rei' endless river of return
from the deeply self-concealed clearest Source outflows
Which closely distant - is in dazzling absence unwilling
to have become–even most remotely–narrated
by an ignorance driven hence afraid of death mortal

But these nectar from sunlight sipping vineyards
finely set among the old austere-grey olive groves
once by the shrewd forgotten gods royally bestowed
grew from their legend more mundane than dreamy
to take roots in the young ages' small nurturing source
in the hard soil of marble time sculpted Greece

She still–against the blood-red sunrise–oversees
all her arid goat-friendly floating sky-steep rocks
in times past by a volcano wildly burst alive, apart, torn
Healed since, by vast lofty winds' waving gusts
that haunt sails harshly the with salty foam breathing
At great fleets sinking savvy–Hellenic-blue seas

She lasts along the gravel-coarse bare shoreline
In of words short-terse fishermen'–frugal art adorned
with rows of ancient laceworks anew just the same
Handcrafted of stiff octopi left to hang flat-dried
which at dawn - quick and supple to cruel nets swam
trading safety of darkness–for zeal to catch the sun

Only here in true-Greece's world–smaller and flatter
at the–with cicadas slow pulsing–late unsealed hour
a gap in time-flow resurrects the faint distance muted
proud far songs and by spear cracked bronze's noise
of the gold-power-fame triad chasing
antique dreams' wars
Frozen sounds melting into one's soul uplifting music
that circle dances behind the clean newly whitewashed
with blue gate in lively purple–warmly open walls...

Well guiding from elsewhere to the plain here and now
The brought about by resin–bitterly strong taste
with its crisp Mediterranean breezes' pine-fragrance
again blessing thick glasses of a bit thinner home wine
surely gets–in increments–more refined and nobler
by the next–even broader–smile of good friend

CONVERSATION OF PLANTS–HAPPINESS

A primrose looked for happiness
I feel quite happy over here
protected from the wind and rain
- Explained a pink carnation
I grew much taller than others
and it intoxicates me lately
- Curtly uttered a flying dandelion
Thank you hardworking wind
A drop of water fell on me
- Just thought an unassuming clover

MINIATURES III

Destiny

Into a vase's shape
By the potter's hand instilled
The sound of breaking
Good shoes of blackness
Kept distant by the urge to exist
Slow patient patter

Solitude

As you–in memory's maze
So wind–caressing snowflakes
Cannot find an exit
Cold night–an empty space
Against too-early widowhood
Reaches the farthest stars

This Place

Here–as a little child
I often stopped with my mother
Long passed away
Why do I find
While aimlessly wandering
This place–again?

THE TEACHING BIRD

The common teaching bird
likely on purpose
Hides its nest–yet close enough
So one willing to learn
quite easily could

This nest is neither too small
nor naively oversized
Always frugal and organic

It carefully plans the future
Warming the eggs
with its own renewable energy
Green true economic

It attacks no one
but defends its nest skilfully
Though at first
only with the warning war cry

It reliably offers the hatchlings
simply what they need
seldom a bit more
and never provides excess

It just knows not
of overkill harmful attachment
so lets them leave on time
to fly their own way

The plain teaching bird
doesn't seem to grasp the concept
of feeling sorry for oneself
Even–while it dies

FAREWELL

in memory of Urszula Poplawski

The last sunset farewell–to a land old facing deluge–
Sang by cantabile cicadas' crisp-dry monotonous choirs

Proudly the pyramids' peaks plough their red-cloudy fields
But the dogs howl and squads of birds form frantically fast

As the evening port street noises–gradually die down
Why temples won't stop pounding these huge sacred drums?

Despite–the sound of bracelets at last comes–long awaited
A warm whisper leads laughter deep into lush garden…

When a sudden wind overpowers the calm shores' andante
The running girl's speeding sandals dance her last staccato

For its youthfully keen white magic with love's act rewarded
A happy flute has awakened the dead eyes in stone statues

Unlucky stars. Behind the sleeping city's night-eclipsed walls
The sea cold power and the might of sands have conspired…

THE PASSAGE FOR VIOLIN

Like musical string instruments
with the tuning mental bows
We play stars' notes the universe wrote
Likewise–musical seems the reason
for the likely spellbinding by beauty
and natural magnetic attraction
at times almost painfully felt
when the universal quasi-opposites
start approaching each other
directly–and dreamlike fleetingly–
before their dramatic crossover
to new fusion in sudden harmony

Such feeling may possibly arise
when dusk retires blending into night
As darkness re-enters its early light
while a walking valley slows the fast pace
seeking to rest in air-born shades
of its silver-edged mountain ranges
or–the sun sprinkled dry shores
open with warm sands to chilly seas

This clearly distinct–subtly elating
yet vaguely sad in depth feeling
might be the mystery-veiled anticipation
of that purposeful while nostalgic
ghostly crossover secret passage
carved in void tunnel through which
friendly helped by the loyal death
that guides us impartially wise
Life crosses the border as known to itself

to then–invisible like a thought–
return some when as nearly different
Old violin music–played anew

THE OLD STONE HOUSE
for Alona Poplawski

Here an orchard once grew…
Behind the crumbling wall
Now fruitless tree turns wild

The abandoned old tools
have given way to labours
of slow hardworking rust

Long the people are gone…
in the mute-empty stone house
A wasps' dry nest lives only

Have those far laughs and cries
become few hidden notes
in the same wind's melody?

THE PUMA PUNKU RUINS–BOLIVIA

The punishing bright edge
and stark anonymous demise
Unmistakably
Have both become petrified here
In the abruptly executed
domino effect
by the precisely cut rectangular stones
of the Baalbec Rock's
staggering kind

Only before–and after
that past proto-epically buried dark event
the shapeless time
must have flown over here
in it's usually predictable
quiet linear way

Then–under the aging sky
the vast Mama Cota's
Mother Lake's
young body of water
over the course of dry millenniums
forlorn by the crossing reed-fleets
refused offerings' gifts
deprived of fishermen chants
receded in part
into azure thin air

On Titicaca Lake's now barren
steep terraced shores
the stepping narrow fields not tended to
retained to no avail
by the ancient stone walls
instead of with cold stunted potatoes
Endlessly bear
at this sub-icy altitude
The arid grey melancholy
Solemn
Andean-hard

BETWEEN HEAVEN AND EARTH

for Tamara Reasin

When the third cycle neared its violent end, the once gentle Titans blindly ventured to offend Gods. Despite wavy golden or red hair and the towering fallen-angelic good looks, they became the brazen, insatiable, embarrassing embodiment of what Gods hated to love about their own past secret sins. No wonder that Gods' wisdom had unravelled, and raged at its very craftiest for the last forty days of the pre-epic clash. The provoked oceans rose, bringing healing relief for their former long dry bottoms, shaking in painful seizures.

The already shrunk, less mobile Titans, in the last wild roars, cursed their merciless parents, the hellish overcast heavens, and soon vanished with the victimized by them, colluding spellbound Dwarfs. As dense sediments settled, the nomadic colourful species came via the gigantic portals, to claim the ruined palaces and temples.

Some Titans though, who inhabited the high ground's military outposts, in steely desperation, built their refuge from the slabs of hardened fire they disguised as the eerily precise cut to fit, enormous polished stones. They hid the last-stand fortress between heaven and earth, craving to continue for as long as they could, with the now simplified astronomical, and sad carnal rituals involving the precious few Titanic females left.

The all-seeing Gods, who calmed down after exerting that much wrath, still made the difficult collective decision to unleash their feared jaguars in the form of disc-shaped swift condors. One fateful hour they swept suddenly out of thin air, swooping from behind the peak of the puzzlingly beautiful steep green mountain. After rapidly melting the roofs and upper walls, the Gods' unforgiving lightning did incept the reign of the incredibly long pristine silence.

For innumerable circles, with which the mourning planet ritually danced at slow pace, anchored to its giant bonfire, only the endlessly waving luminous ribbons of the migratory birds flew over the forlorn ruin. The self-contained, differently wise wild animals avoided the place not bothering to know why. Meantime, the fourth cycle had emerged in the fresh force of its youthful dawn. The surviving Dwarfs, as all the other small short-lived beings, have successfully multiplied, as the quickly aging generations passed in a twinkling of the all-seeing blue eye. The oldest memories faded and left, except for the archetypal fear of something too elusive to name–one mustn't talk about, buried in the darkest past.

The agile Dwarfs' mercurial curiosity, and their keen desire for comfort, inevitably overcame their tantalizing fears. The boldest ones left the scorching heat of the desert, or the scary jungle steaming with venal snakes, and lit their tiny fires in the murky shade of the overwhelmingly colossal foundations.

Much later, the venerated throughout lush fertile valleys and sombre mountain ranges the cast away Giant Viracocha, ordered their descendents to add to the walls of the mighty ruins the biggest stones they could cut and lift. Then, with a light smile on his huge regular face, he told them to claim the site as their own in live festivities, full of corn beer craze, cheery dances, and the nostalgically harmonious, antediluvian music of the immortal flutes and drums.

Much later still, the last descendents of the post-Phoenician bloodline king, who strived to be remembered as Inca, sought in their stoic desperation to hide the haunted place between heaven and earth again. They learned from their best spies that as the short foreign Gods, commanding some small thunderous lightning, un-wrap the hard pure-silver cocoons at night, they do not convert to heavenly gadflies, but have deeply troubling dreams.

So not unwisely, they came to believe that the fourth cycle nears its cleansing end preceding the next renewal, and were perhaps mistaken only by few hundred circles of the silent planet's slow ritual dance around the sacred golden or red bonfire burning out patiently.

THE EGO MATRIX

It might be–with some fine arts' license–submitted
that this world reminds one of a self-solving puzzle
slowly circling its set continuum–
probably from Alpha to Omega

No wonder that the more subtly important
small universe
of one's quick fragile and thin-legged ego
weaves and traverses the concentric web
of continuums on its own

It appears as if each continuum on such a web
by some clever design maintains
its punishing extreme temperature
on both blind edges–seemingly juxtaposed

Possibly–the most life-consuming among all trajectories
is precariously far overstretched
from the pale-dark blaze of hate
to the dark-pale flame of mad love

It has been taught by the planet's elders that to follow
the sirens' hypnotic song of any extremes
remains destructive for the earthlings
if with a few noble exceptions

So somewhere in the much safer
since ego-temperate zone
the ancient social art of warm true friendship
set a mature garden for those
from the web's maze-phase retired

TO BE ONESELF

in memory of Gad Czudner, correctional psychologist

The plain applied morality does present itself–as is
in a coarse but warm self-confident voice
with the richly rendered Israeli accent
For it grew in a kibbutz of the promised new sunrise
in the sparse holy land of hard work and prayers
under the shade of–on sands erected–hope

The "nobody's fool" brusque morality naturally sees
to stay put–it does not know any better–
While trespassing on the foreign to it domain
of the Alice's in Wonderland
obliquely bent corridors
where the relative yes might amount to no
and the no strives under the wing of half-opened yes

With the driest self-depreciating sense of humor
that conceals the thick-skinned finesse
it simply shares itself with the re-condemned ones
whether they mockingly giggle at it
behind its broad shoulder
or–not yet knowing why–do come closer
form a group in a tattooed circle
starting to listen up with a budding respect

The straightforward kibbutz born morality
can–why not–suddenly visit
the by life's light forlorn newly widowed man
to naively say in its noble heart first aid
- Cheer up now my old friend
I may have found you a nice new wife

It can on time complete the wise off beat
by readers forgotten before published
self-help book on the home practice of base morality
For those parents by fear petrified
who look at their offspring–life's meaning deprived
facing the high risk of the inner voice loss

The tough–all set to sail morality–a compass itself
or to life sentenced scroll in the
now to dust breaking jar
in a matter of fact way does the chore of illness
works the death task masterly well
as a good tool's hardened blade
the one made of diamond–in the finest of rough

THE SCALE OF SUCCESS

Within the most brilliant rocket ever launched
by esteemed social sciences
being a bold scale from zero towards ten
the range of sober realism
- set on the continuum
from the unrealistic pessimism
to the equally unrealistic rosy optimism–
seems to assert itself somewhere around five

This particular range
by definition should be the one most desirable
for anyone preparing their own success

The lower zone–below five
properly hosts the sadly unrealistic pessimists
duly bound to under-perform
yet for whatever obscurely illogical reason
that high–off realism–
range of the incurable optimists
the one much above five
invariably features the "en passant" winners

AN INTEGRITY TEST

The first ever Integrity Test
[Still to be validated and standardized]
in psychology history
comes in the elaborated
three distinctly diagnostic steps

The introductory one
evaluates the ability to instantly refuse
any life's time golden opportunity
if remotely compromised

The second–harder step
assesses the aptitude for the unwavering
loyalty to those past values
of own teachers who already left

The final and toughest subtest
a handful passes–probes the capacity
of willing to clinically die
for the values in question

This subtest however
not yet fine-tuned thus least diagnostic
at present stage doesn't rule out
the acute depressives
let alone the honest fanatics

TWO PRISONS

for Chaplain Wayne Moore

To become a part of the outer prison
would pretty much pre-require
constructing that own inner one–first

All the right building materials
come free–available as readily
as poor thoughts and feelings acted upon

Surely some surrounding others
casually nourish them all too well
for the good reason of just-because

Once built with such confused help
that complex lone inner prison
sets-in behind the mute barb-wired walls

They just cannot open until the day
when the cold bitterly sad phantom-jail
falls under its own unbearable weight

PSYCH–WARD
for Duncan Scott, MD

They feel the way we all do
it's just slashed their wrists
with what remains hidden
between possible and impossible

Flatly–or dramatically
they offer others precious little
yet continue to invite in
too much homeless space

They grew afraid as all of us
except they gazed at the inner abyss
so brazenly close to it
that it started leering at them

EXTREME PERSONALITY–OBSESSIVE-COMPULSIVE

It is too difficult to keep in check
that un-definable cloud
of vague anxiety
and live constantly harassed
by the cold whisper
from my invisible internal world

Fortunately for me
the external thus tangible world
stays definitely easier
to relate to and manage perfectly

For instance
I can–plausibly–teach my hands
to wash and wash themselves
until they approach
the desirably ideal extreme

Any aimed target of my attention
may become controlled
by the constantly applied
hence repetitively returning focus
reliably change-proof

Even every seventh lantern
on each proper street
can be long-term trained
to have me circling it times three
Before my regular walk
completes in relief

Realize please - just in case
only as long as someone
would not attempt to compromise
this tightly impeccable order
I've arranged for
I stay quietly–sort of nice

EXTREME PERSONALITY–SCHIZOID

If you naively assume
that I must shiver
in the–by your standards–
icy and barren
world of mine
You are dead wrong
It suits my needs just fine

Besides–
Let's now get it straight
I am genuinely
uninterested to pretend
that I care at all
what you might ponder
about me
freezing in my world

Do not get me wrong
At a certain level
I do suspect
that behind the cold glass
in your world
the temperature
might be slightly milder
weather a bit better

But once I envision
your endless chitchatting
behind this glass
Your smiles' exchanges
and that ritual
of an eye contact
All do make me
to snug in my own igloo

EXTREME PERSONALITY–SCHIZOTYPAL

Some space around me discloses special signs
which others–do not even appear to detect
or wrongly do not consider them to be meaningful

Yet–I must decipher those cryptic messages
For interpreting all of them in my peculiar way
which others do not seem to - really appreciate
or sadly–do not perceive them as being of value

I strive to finally find that key concealed too well
for unlocking the mystery and become fulfilled
before the next signs or messages would appear...

EXTREME PERSONALITY–AVOIDANT

Given a scope of my new challenge
I know what to expect
And taking all of it into account
I would rather not go

Even if I did not feel good
not showing up there
Sure I could feel worse if I would
So–why bother?

I would disappoint everybody there
Starting with myself
Here–my ego doesn't run a risk
only feels kind of sour
about itself

Then again
Does anyone ever
feel that great about one's
self-aborted performance
that–otherwise–could have been
just - perfect?

Finally–all in all–
Prudently choosing the lesser evil
under the circumstances
does not amount anyway
to avoiding scrutiny
too morbidly

EXTREME PERSONALITY–PASSIVE-AGGRESSIVE

A life of a quiet exploited man
Could reach its highest point
When the long pent-up feelings
Of enough explode in–*enough*

Then all the elaborated systems
of the entitled harsh oppression
are surely bound to collapse

Mahatma Ghandi did prove that
for the sake of human justice
so did good Martin Luther King

I'm not yet able–at this point–
to hone my budding charisma
in such esteemed big leagues
but do know my stuff well indeed

Adapting their peaceful method
I–do not fight authority at work
or that bossing one at home
in any violent too mean a way

Instead–I would dawdle, mislead
sabotage, and again procrastinate
while grudgingly quasi-agreeing
with my detectably tired oppressor

If only all other good people
would follow my insightful lead
world's hot wars could be ending
in the frosty vinegar-sour truce

EXTREME PERSONALITY–BORDERLINE

Is my maiden name Borderline?
Well–that may precisely be why
I ever tensely love but hate you
Either–just plainly, respectively,
Or masterly at the very same time

I am not quite sure as we speak
Where to–my last border has left
Something does keep erasing it
Are you surprised I grew this mad?

If you abandon me be fully aware
I could readily slash myself bad
Perhaps instead hurt you good
Or–even much better–do both

I demand plenty of your attention
But you–from now on will require
a new passport for that crossing
of my border–one fluid again
far pushed by your stupid little help

EXTREME PERSONALITY–HISTRIONIC

My portable stage soon rises anywhere I go
since my potential audience
In fact–incorporates anyone I relate to

I work hard towards capturing that audience
with the only method I know
sometimes playing a black comedy
but preferably staging the evolving dramas

Performing consumed by this creative play
I verbally act out the unfolding drama
of almost every situation
challenging me in my uniquely shaping life

I feel so much better about myself
when my good audience pays due attention
otherwise my fragile feelings splinter

Yet you had better never expect
any–dramatic or not–friendship from me
Once you try to be a critic of my theatre
I–talk only to the sentient audience

EXTREME PERSONALITY–NARCISSISTIC

My important - and first of all–undisputable
though impeded by the jealous others
thus potential–contribution to any social surrounding
is to be pronounced in a crystal-clear way
Since my superior skills harnessed by the brilliant mind
have been impossible to match
wherever–albeit briefly–I functioned

In spite of these rare but well deserved gifts
the very core of the true me remains painfully uncertain
To be honest–pervasively anxious
All too often to quite menacing a point
of–ironically–feeling bad about myself

Under no circumstances however
would I let anybody exploit
that deep chronic sentiment
Whoever cresses eggshells to touch my thin skin
will surely end up as all my attackers well attended to
be forewarned then and never–I mean never ever
dare to utter that word "narcissistic" again
in front of the So-Special *me*

EXTREME PERSONALITY–PARANOID

I do not know what others whisper about me
But do feel they plot–even much worse

Some of them have been venally devious
Perhaps that's why they pose as my friends

They sure plan to hurt me in their dark ways
Believing I would underestimate the threat

I remain gravely afraid–if deeply inside
But they also had better be and very much so...

Now I have to constantly scan my perimeters
Where their "surprise" attack will come from

They come mad-fanatical–acutely paranoid
Have I multiplied them in my self-defence

EXTREME PERSONALITY–DEPENDENT

As far I can only remember
While hearing those others talking
on the same flat floor I stood too
I have always somehow felt
that others' part of that floor has been
more elevated than my spot

Accordingly–to be at last able to properly
interact with all of them
in a way naturally I began to look up
even though many of them were
obviously much shorter than me

As a consequence–I guess–
I've submitted the power of attorney
over making decisions in my life
to the various consecutive representatives of others
so they have been ever since consistently
micromanaging it for me

Could anyone explain to me as to why–
all of them have invariably given me back
instead of some gratitude
their oblivious fleeting disrespect
when they've catered to about everyone else but me?

The truth is that for some unknown
and nearly paralyzing me reason
I am–I guess–unable to go it just alone
and harbour my strength-draining fear

whether I could make it independently
in this too chilly for me world

Such bad feelings do freeze me
to the lone core of my trembling being
so that daily bread of disrespect–or often much worse
is the inflated price I cannot stop paying I guess
Can I? Moreover–they promised to change…

EXTREME PERSONALITY–MIXED

If you call me mixed-up
I may–legally–take an action
Since my elusively set personality
has been "diagnosed"
exclusively–as Mixed

Unlike the competition
I do not muster just one specialty
Being aptly prolific
in my various features or traits
misconstrued as "symptoms"

These traits {not symptoms}
may not be as clearly pronounced
as among my competition
At least–I keep them
reasonably unpredictable

Just attempt to probe me
expecting a tense paranoid response
I would take you by surprise
with a schizoid shy smile

Or–you may try to console
the dependent part in me
I could fiercely reject your efforts
in a snap-narcissistic rage

Could you–please
at last figure out my own labyrinth
to find where I "got lost"?
Don't you worry–just kidding…

EXTREME PERSONALITY–PSYCHOPATH

My–coldly scanning yours–mind
works as an inherent part of true nature
not unlike one of a forest or a lake
also–of your cute tidy-sweet garden

All what lives there devours the inferior
since to prevail–therefore to thrive
each dweller of those pristine habitats
by own nature does–whatever it takes

Don't call my way the path of a psycho
Stop jumping to these false conclusions
so conveniently–not once admitting
to full normalcy of just consistent me

Come on–return at last to your senses
you are merely a prey trespassing - my turf
and ought much more appreciate myself
who does not fake to be–someone else

Ok–I'll give that to you I pretend a lot
But whether a funny chameleon does not
or that crafty hence white-bellied shark
not seen from below–before it strikes?

Why do you seem to act as afraid of me?
I am honestly interested in harvesting you
I try to develop some sense of humor
and trust me–have great stories to tell...

DRUG ADDICTION

for Kathy Bales, addiction counsellor

It is easy for one to spit at me
But if–you–had to listen
to that one sound
that saddest cry in angry roar
of something
wrapped in the black fog
deep–in yourself
You could be a fugitive like me

I am doing my faulty best to flee
from that sound
via the escape-route I've found
as an effort-demanding ways
have never been
of choice–in a life of mine

After barely–escaping from
I got–shackled to
but you will never become able
to even remotely grasp
how good it feels
oh how sweet it feels
to see those diamonds in the sky

For quickly looking at them again
I would instantly do
just about anything forbidden
I've got trapped–
I cannot listen to that sound
and cannot stop
Reaching for my diamonds…

POWER ADDICTION

It is now–or never
soaring to that intoxicating top
above the hungry streets
Their rage just spelled out
Blood currency spent
for the common cause
Wishfully perceived
Flying as high
and as much solo as it gets
above the mass' songs of hope
But never as a junkie-moth
to its flame addicted
rather–an eagle-hero
one stately modest
holding a benign sunbeam
in claws of might

While rapidly soaring
to crown and consecrate own ego
assemble the entourage
contrive good punishments
promise paradise now
But–perhaps a bit later
hypnotize the crowds with "I'm-you"
then use–use daily
Gliding craftier than Icarus
Yet despite
–at last–getting high
to feel so afraid
of other wings' mortal swoop
as to justly distribute

own torturous fear
long time before
the overdue immolation

Being birth marked
with the letters A and H
heralding a quite unassuming alias
The family covert name
boasting over the ages
Not just one only
but the two–gothic-sharp T's

"To be defeated not yielding is victory."
—Marshall Jozef Pilsudski

A BATTLE IN THE HOLOCAUST
for Janus Avivson

When–death foretelling–stark intuition
in silence looks at the last fallen
ditch of staunch denial
One true ally–yet to shoulder standing
may just be firm deeply entrenched hope

Once hope dies–wounded by cruel reality
The stern force of personal courage
could resist alone
Fed on the inner Masada's war-cry and prayer
God–Adonai–let my battle conclude in pride

If still holding the line courage–begins to retreat
pushed back by cyclone-armed orderly torture
Perhaps one's pure flame-like yearning
of return into calmly approaching
eternal unknown
now might bring the invisible aid

Before the torn body gets burnt essence-less
the free unbroken commanding post
of a soul's integrity
could have been defended by its naked will
until the unknown–flown home
on a shield of ash–victory
over unleashed cold hell–beaten at life's cost…

THE GHETTO RISES

for Rabbi Marc Gellman

…and somewhere high
above the land un-promised
reach us with the murmur
of their prayers
Marc Chagall's
And Marc Gellman's
un-aspiring saints
by blinding smoke veiled
flying martyred
in the thorniest of air…

…somewhere faraway
cut off by the day's gate
behind the cruel walls of night
falling–rises
a yellow star–the brave…

MINIATURES IV

Beyond Words

For those few dead-like
who emerged from the steel Leviathan
of Holocaust
Nothing must have felt real
except a number tattooed on their visceral courage
The abysmal smell of saddest victory
as if the moral backbone of humanity
still smoldered

Alms

It feels as though
on the fire's edge
with the softest of blue
somebody's
sadly lone arms
in hunger endless
ask for love's sparse alms...

Poetic Bird

Out of thousands of birds
following thousands
one only might become–poetic
To own devices left
of the bell towers
and night watchtowers'–owl the poor
circles gliding before its death
and after

FRANZ KAFKA

To find the seed of the darkest wind
that blows simultaneously
from the East North West and South
over subdued landscapes
one presumably could
not unlike the Golem's gifted master
be in the cold-eerie dreams visited
by the un-golden ghosts
haunting medieval cemeteries
of the midnight-grey Prague

For the painful reshaping
of own mind–to a precise diapason
one among the few most receptive
But just by that uniquely sophisticated
indispensable tone finer
it probably wouldn't hurt to be born
a feather-thin Wandering Jew

Nevertheless–
To vivisect such proud civilization
via genius so compulsive
as to create the subtlest satire ever
on the self-crowned species
Then–with a smirk–conceal
dry humor behind the blackest of drama
all for opting to quasi-hide
the core of his opus magnum from humans
in Max Brod's conscience
One surely must have
come here from the far elsewhere
only as poor Franz

"Cast a cold eye on life and death. Horsemen pass by."
-William B. Yeats

DISCLOSURE
for Andrzej Klinowski

Even though mine impermanent tight corset of a body
stays confined to time and space–if only for a while–
The edge probing altered mind indeed wouldn't stop
- Safe in its frost-proof clarity's capsule natural of me -
to dive down the icy vacuum both space-less and timeless
Where the seemingly dead Punic wars go on just as close
as the warlike in slow motion unfolding sequences
of baby-steps to prompt this young planet's pre-unification
overlapped by the battles of Trafalgar and Stalingrad

The plainly visible leaders in fine brushed cylinders
bespectacled moustache-armed en vogue goatee-bearded
with birdlike fast though not too funny movements
lurking behind the mute dark-grey documentaries
last–not at all less consequential powerful and epic
than those hip–in color smiling lured to elite's planes
to–on a roll jog - down the crimson-royal carpets
and also than the adult ones in white togas soft sandals
who wear alien headdresses–on long skulls nobly pointed
For all are real enough thus equally heed-worthy to me

The never sunken Atlantis' walls built by the tall race
I sense to be as present as the lost sweet-crude civilization
and Leonardo's dry military sketches dagger sharp
bring the similar focus in me as the multiple warheads
jovially peddled to inland shepherds of submerged flocks
Also an awe-inspiring the very first print of Guttenberg
I find just as breathtaking as a computer cells' plasma
Even tour de force coup of the modern depth thinkers
attracts me no sooner than Gobi Desert's scars
–turned glass ...

THE UPDATE

The oldest deft foes–earth water and fire
still conspire to break the fleeting truce
of the last twelve thousands earth-circles
Re-plotting anew a holy clash of elements

Yet the grand illusion of quaint times
continues to cast here calm innocent spell
So the frail dusk–blending into darkness
returns in a radiant mask of the next dawn

The compact globe remains safely flat
with its universe proper–circling around
For the fierce old tribes that fast grow apart
and start to sharpen momentum's thin blade

SEMANTICS–RELIGION

We are raised in varied languages
of old tribes warring well
on continents of a planet far off The Central Way
In our ethos–mere signs of religions
blind the over-zealous
to make sad choices over life or death

True graciously can shine a good common tool
Cutting a precious slice of bread–with respect offered
to a stranger in need–invited indoors

What a tragically final object it becomes
if it pierces the young unsuspecting–
with life beating heart
thus forces a soul to - in horror–depart

Like a two-sided value of one coin–
the vast magic of atom
may either nurture–basking in peace–cities
or transcend them in seconds into wind-blown ash

Religion may become–at times–the misused best tool
with the most potent power for our true growth
the tool written for–but read and
applied by the so young us…

This energy-tool–the roadmap to the Absolute
if marred with lone fears
uniting themselves through hatred
then extorted by the swollen egos lusting to expand
may change to a sword the one starkly pointing
to history torture-chambers of hell yet to pass

The gift of religion–the noblest energy and tool in one
is able to trigger tremors fomenting
the greatest collapses…

Yet ultimately–only its pure essence can unite
the new ourselves–yesterday's adolescents
facing adulthood
For serving maturely tenderness and care
at the pleasure of soon emerging
One Light in all it suns…

"Humans are the toys of gods."
—An ancient proverb

THE CURRICULUM

History lives comprised of stealth inching slowly
Socio-tectonic plates beneath its surface dust
on which deep fault lines juxtaposed we stand
While they re-start to tremble–compressed again
to trigger the patiently evolving war-tremor
of monuments-spawning–thus epic proportions

Perceived as natural–by gods surveyed fault lines
wait buried under time layers sleeping soundly
until the world's stage gets revolved to precisely fit
The next pan-cleansing spillage of sin-burning lava
to affirm the bestowed religions' fundamental creed
of Heaven wrath–at the child-human dark side

AFAR AT THE TOO-YOUNG AGE

for Geoff Hutchinson

Lightning with thunder
by flames reopen
silence's gate

Above the dust cloud
few sand grains light bound
wait for return

Joy stricken scorpions
hail desert's shelter
in a broken helmet

Mighty avalanche
of car advertisements
covers short news

***

No use to cry–mom
why hug in vain
that spring apple tree?

Stay strong like me
serving the weak
walked not talked the walk

Once trusted in lofty talk…

Power–earns penny…
I chose a pound as I fell down
giving his life to a friend

I stood up to his death
straight face to face
enforced it to go through me

Now tough came orders
“Spot frozen stars
and melt them with your heart”

I’ve got to go far…

Reshaped into light
I’ll once return to you
A warm sunspot on grieving doors

MINIATURES V

Sacrifice
in memory of Witold Poplawski Senior

Where the silk-soft falling petals
decorated my uniform torn
red poppies grow under a pale sun
Dandelions' weightless parachute
above the sacrificial altars
to the die-hard wars of human kind

Summary

They–got defined
by Acropolis and Spartans' Gorge
The bright chisel of Fidias
We'll be tallied up
by the rust of debris sad Guernica
A cicada blade's song

Question

We–
The seamen tired
of fighting high wind and themselves
now ask our miniature hearts
as the journey concludes
Where this due port will be–
In the nucleus of darkness
Or light?

ON ST. ELM'S SEA

Emerged from fire of their birth-pangs
–predestined fragilities
God's clock-run round creations
spin in time through space
ending circular flights in flames
of inferno for spawning new worlds

One not-alone traveler reminds of a blue ship
under torn sail of clouds
struggling at the sheer and forever
un-tangibly executed mercy
of its not-to-be-chartered boundless waters
–vast bottomless love

Whatever storms at dawn destroy
on rough deck nutshell-thin
The sun-lit zealous noon with its childlike trust rebuilds
for the needy waves which return upon
the brewing shades of dusk

Most sailors long forgot the true essence
of their whereabouts
believing that they rest safe
and aye-aye sound in due port
Mistaking the grey-green shapes and lights
for benign sunrays

All are endlessly in fighting–
some hatch the odd holy mutinies
looking for that real captain–with unimpeded foresight–
Yet replacing the stark-selfish ones
with some new–even blinder

At nights the on duty watchman whispers
from the fog-shrouded mast
that the invisible rescue armada–one just undreamt of–
still races with the unfathomed Maelstrom
–no one sees ahead

ARMAGEDDON

in memory of Andrzej Bursa, Cracow's forgotten true poet

The dire events have quickly unfolded almost as prophesized. After the state astrologers and non-conspiracy theorists divined the ominous economic forecast, the people of gold

started pondering about food, those with food over gold, many about water, and even more took naps. The bone-dry shamans from the world's fourth dimension squatted in their bushy huts, and with the vitriolic political incorrectness wryly hissed that Mother Earth has become mad for being greedily abused, and soon will respond in her wild fury.

Moreover, the polls consistently indicated that if things ever went this far, the healthy majority would be willing to watch Armageddon live on TV, if ably hosted by the adored personalities in Armagedroom. The global in-depth survey, via the least un-trusted news, revealed that the show down chosen snacks would be popcorn for the home theatres, and

the dates in honey for the smaller dim screens; coca chewers flatly opted out. Now a pharmaceutical giant brilliantly introduced Aspiriddon, a derivative from the extremely potent medieval end of the world potion, despite its proven side effect of myopia. Under the mounting duress there was not much choice left. The visible rulers got a nod to get on with the protocol, and charmingly conducted the entry ceremony of cordial declarations.

In a historic goodwill gesture they even exchanged tin soldiers' heirloom collections, hiding behind the white orchids their real emotions seductively. Subsequently, the solemn inner envoy submitted on a black lacework-pillow the long awaited final proof.

In an updated ancient ritual, the sacrosanct flame o fear-turned-noble-wrath got gently re-lit by a cultured geo-philosopher in front of a richly framed media-worthy icon, held close to the war chest by a sweet-crude visionary. Soon the light-footed troops of the platinum - tongued psych-oopsologists in daily lofty lyrics reduced the enemy to venomous seals, so one would feel deeper and try harder if at cull.

The granite-faced rear commander, who never blinked under the hostile fire of the armoured wall piercing explosive memos, dryly ensured that usual supplies will be enhanced with the courts-on-wheels to support field legions. Giggly militant kids were already blowing bridges and serially killing the invaders in the hastily issued to them defensive videogames.

In turn, the amassed armies of adult warriors sang in tears the powerful old songs about the vast beauty of their respective lands, creed purity, and the glory of superb ancestral combat. Afterwards, they skilfully adorned the riding and flying chariots, painting on the metal surfaces frightening large heads of the alerted predatory birds or fish. Their shiny spears, bullets, axes, and rockets instantly turned laser-sharp and evil-focused.

Then, in sudden silence, they slowly began putting the colors of rotting plants and of soil on their rapidly sweating faces. Armageddon was about to unveil. A few yet un-uniformed women looked above in terror, as the aimed asteroid was said to be approaching fast. Its menacing dark harbinger, a huge crescent-like shape, was seen for seven nights on the southern skies.

The next midnight the madly clever three-headed dragon Belsebaal from eastern hell was born on Earth. The sheer gravity of the situation at last woke up the underground sleeper-boards that anew tried to interpret less secret dreams to their forgetful surface societies, alas leaving them in juxtaposed confusion. Yet, to the total surprise of all, the unforeseen did strike.

Without warning everything has eerily changed. The horror was gone. There was no Armageddon. Instead, a poor bloody super-regional war, with strong growth potential, was breaking in due instalments out. Albeit the matter had clarified itself just fine, the oddly vague but robust rumors have continue to persist, that Armageddon will now be almost fully allowed, after the seven long years of soon to be enjoyed new peace

HURRICANE CAME

Home–surrounds its adult child
Like a mother
Like a cradle
Giving slowly way to world

It would rather tame that world
with own doors and windows

But the helpless world does come
through the walls
through the roof
Bringing wind then moonlight

From now on
what home means
a mute chill will be explaining
the deaf homeless road

THE PRAYER OF HIOB

YOU–The Ultimate Incognito

Of all the deterring walls' doors
opening on time Constructor

In the long pauses of our pulse
The Entity–homeless immensely

In-trance clairvoyant Self-Being
evolving myriads of new eyes

Of Your perpetuating joy-enigma
A triad: The Author Witness and Aim

Let us sooner that You've dreamt of
Hear and see from the dust rise…

THE GRAND SCHEME OF THINGS

for Eugene Stasiak

The timid mere potential for Good
A tiny nucleus of light pre-conceived to grow
starts–left on the universe's bottom–
like newborn infant omni-vulnerable
terrified of the abruptly denser abode

This is where it meets entitled Evil
Endures its blind self-serving power
in the small hence painful scheme of things
Mercifully–only in between–
Short and in vain dreaded beneficial breaks

In such arduous but not endless way
It gradually grows its cosmic claws and teeth
forced to juxtapose in strain
Self-define learning to shield the weaker
For Good falters as its own hazy shade
until gets of self-might–precisely aware

While suffering yet evolving in agony
The still-afraid future Good commits countless
Cruel despicable deeds–of itself
Before it's at first self- absorbed perception
With sprouting love refocuses on others
Then hears the true call beyond the native stars

Freed to become–it does not need relating
to the insatiably myopic Evil anymore
As just like the speed of home returning light
It leaves its crystallized in black ex-tormentor
Dimensions further–than far behind

The highest power in the mature Good
chooses not to destroy the inept to rule Evil
shackled to the red-hot iron ball of false pride
Rather–if to a measured degree–
seeks to harness its dark confused usefulness
for those hardest lessons of entry
of the newly born children of light

LIFE TALKS

Relentlessly looking at me
for all this long time–
What are you?

As a matter of hard fact
I am your own life

Have come from mystery
Belong elsewhere
Yet depend–on you

Your changing perceptions
clearly maintain
all my characteristics

Once you see me as ugly
So be it indeed
If cruelly unbearable–
Count on that too

Want to terminate me then?
I'll take you alright
By the wildest surprise
Of… your life

Live me - despite?
Sure–relax figure out focus
and gladly follow
my natural order

Think I am overly complex?
I am plain genial
so must remain simple

You may as well consider
to begin learning
how to respect and love me
After all
you do not seem to have
that much choice

But before starting just look
straight in my eyes–
to sense what glows within…

HUMAN INNER GROWTH

Human's inner growth
if an abstract commodity only–
does properly carry
its adequately set price

Both on individual growth plan
and on a group one
The hard currency is expected
with no exceptions made

All instalments must be paid off
When the human growth
Is just about
Reasonably completed

The system relies
on the pay-as-you-go scheme
It's hard currency being
always too-unbearable suffering

Yet–to procrastinate investing it
for due growth potential
means to handsomely increase
the future suffering

Human's true inner growth
some soothing payment holidays
eased up with
needs to simply be suffered through

This checks and balances system
clear and impartial
still remains rewarding though
as our existence proves

THE MIRROR UNIVERSE

for Tadeusz Swidzinski

In wise brilliantly simple
complexity
this part of the universe
that now allows me to perceive it
smiles–as soon as I do

Seemingly
it also hates me at times
Provided my very own trap of hate
I've constructed
painstakingly well

This part of the universe
showing a perfect sense of humor
laughs with spooky grimaces
At me–a tiny wizard
Making faces

However–
It will surely return love
if my dormant emotion's dry seed
sprouts and evolves
As long as I would mean
What I feel

Perhaps at that
from afar still un-fathomed
Awe–of my final journey end–
The best of time will come
To better live the universe
Behind

For–no more distant
in bliss may open
Its lasting dream's sealed interior
All sentient infinite
Sheerest solitude
The pristine Mind Beyond

THE AQUARIUM

for Anna Poplawska

I am a tiny fish
inside the projected by my mind
aquarium of air

I humbly live
on oxygen steady flow and daily
organic staples

By each breath
something extends my fish-life
in a free gift

It also leaves
fresh food's succulent spectrum
close to my lips

So I pay it back
trying to exhale good thoughts
calm feelings

SEMANTICS–RACE

Before new knowledge becomes wisdom
that finds through love the path beyond
the readiness exam prepared for humans
involves an entry test as practice shows

Without the "visibly different" races
there couldn't come this helpful chance
of voiding our acute misperception
thus learning to see the diverse - as one

How could we–even remotely–greet
all-diversity realms in outer space
Not at first training ourselves - here
in the non-judging our neighbours' races

We strive to reach beyond ourselves
before we might be touching the stars afar
That's why all races were given in us
so the first exam could in hard steps start…

THE LONG-TERM GAME

for Suzan Gleeson

With focused goal-aimed mind
provided one walks deftly
in the often differently sized shoes
of the encountered others
and quells mutinies of one's own will
The novice game with the visible parts
of life's complexity
quite likely can be won

But the covert superior player
that stealth-faced no nonsense part
understood as death
does appear to reign invincibly
Never making mistakes
Entirely impossible to measure up to

Incredibly–this most masterful
Of all the shapeless universal players–
could be prevailed upon
Yet only through completed
even in sleep felt
profound love of the Absolute
amongst the top human abilities
The very one
utterly difficult to develop

No wonder that this cause and effect
longest-term individual game
is lost again and again
and - again…

Maybe a chance to ever win
Begins with finely carved in one's mind
and lived by–sentient humility
presumably
a self-prescribed daily dose
of ego-downsizing sense of humor
might become
a shrewd opening movement

THE SAFER PATH

Climbing this cloudy mountain
It could prove more prudent
to adopt a honest belief
than attempt to "understand"
At least–as long
as one would believe fully
thus with an open heart

In such a sincere belief
doesn't wait a hidden pain
But there likely could lurk
the teaching well
icy blade of suffering
in the long and hard toiled for
Proud little understanding

Quite ironically though–
that microscopic-kind grasping
after the climax of one's ego
tends to quietly return
towards the reclaimed belief
probably heartfelt
by a climber–now wiser

CONVERSATIONS OF PLANTS–WISDOM

An ivy asked–what wisdom is
I feel wise when others do what I want
hissed a controlling venous fly-trap
Wisdom is to take the best from life
while not hurting others
sighed a delicately fragrant lily
Give everything back and come to ask then
answered–with a light smile–
a dry high mountain thistle

THE GARDEN OF EDEN

for Richard Tate

Does one's simplest way
to the long speculated on–Garden of Eden
originate in believing?

The dryly-repetitive daily drills of pure logic
tend to deny this route's credibility
let alone any viability

However–
to espouse the five senses' "hard-logical"
does–logically–pre-require
believing in logic

Apparently–no one
manages to somehow go around
the behind-the-scenes high rule of belief

There exists just one mindset though
which in a side effect
renders that rule obsolete

The simple true love towards The Designer
doesn't need anymore
to believe or understand
as it daily tends to the Garden of Eden

THE POWER OF PRAYER

for Rita Tate

In our fast lives that sea-fare ceaselessly
praying–is not just acting if aware
of an access to the radar–left aboard
It is about using its power precisely
lost in the dark among blinding fogs

This universal radar once offered to us
not only beats the edges of black rocks
but from far distance senses the safe port
and leads a ship to the calm of its dock…

THE KEY

The travelling mind–of a soul in journey
reflects its own quick-changing projections
via the so fleetingly passing "deja vu"–
of powers' short array with limited senses
As a result–in good faith all-embraces
what it perceives to be the close material
too-obviously obvious hard-physical world

Within the social more sublime dimension
in that transient world of signs impermanent
A soul long keeps striving to attain a balance
between it's mind and - slow forming - heart...

Yet this heart–the humblest heart only
got a gift of finding via inner voice the key
to the patient in pristine love awaiting
- For a soul that put its clear mind to pure heart -
The Joy-Realm calling in thunderous calm
Revealing itself to the humblest of love
guided by silent light to approach the gate

MINIATURES VI

Our Mothers
in memory of Eugenia Poplawska

... after modest departures
they travel–smaller than a tear–
towards the submerged in blackness
planets–the ones afraid of dark
attempting to cheer them up
with healing phantom-palms
these too good mothers of ours ...

A Campfire

Fast awakened by the dawn's wind frosty
swirl cascading–of gold laurels thin
pre-adorning heaven's rock-clad bottom

An aged wanderer lit his last campfire
for silence reddened by late hilly autumn

Sunrise Sunset

Craving the daylight
within the small world of an eggshell
new eager hatchling

The winged experience
returning through the same star-gate
reopened–at night

"We are the closest to greatness if we are great in humility."
—Rabindranath Tagore

ON THE DEPARTURE OF JOHN PAUL II

Could have the soundless might in the music of time
been ghost offered for this un-perceivably vast temple
- Which seems comprised of rapidly expanding void -
By any other Composer than the dazzlingly unseen?
Then–why did he seem to almost un-veil
asking this humblest of all the rare listeners
for a gift - life's departure in completed harmony?
Why the Musician appears to remain responsive
to even a brief single note of harmony's reflection
felt in birth-to-death-to-birth children lifelong songs?

Which was the oldest of all the unknown reasons
Why The Utter Aim of the profound
saintly-white worship
by this greatest one from the top planetary histrions
- The Aim spawning then growing
endless cosmic dramas
yet hidden by swift powers of It's own scenic masks–
invited this sun-lit worker–to worldwide perform
pointing-out love to the half-innocent
half-awaken audience
that wears their Venetian-like gold-tainted if sad ones
for hubris' hard kernel in fear ridden pride?

With what primal enigma in the design's intention
- For Omega's present circle-journey to re-enter Alpha -
the fragile keen interiors of the living entities' eyes
encrusted in the hard shelters of poly-morphed skulls

became artfully sculpted by the most sentient chisel
enabling these orbs to project both
the shapes and colors
On sheer electro-band multi-mazes of magnetic waves
Then to seek–at the worlds-apart–own differing pace
via a myriad of confusing paths–the same open door?

Is it a blind glance–towards a mountain sealed clue
that the pure Self-Existence of utmost omnipotence
boundless above life and death–identical mortal twins–
remaining thus of no origin–
had felt infinitely orphaned
until for love's sake He sent from self-abyss the sign
Word or Thought
Projecting this spirals' sprung "perpetuum mobile"
a living net woven of black whirling light
knotted by galaxies
to fish with it the depths of endlessly
parallel dimensions
For each droplet of own vested love–ready to return
waiting for that elusive catch in the everywhere
of nowhere
veiled in the silk-soft silence–agelessly intense?

THE INVISIBLE DISC

for Arnold Thomassen

Only the ripe grapevine's age–readying in mid-fall shade
may fully search its life span's loaded info-disc
of the by our world late awarded penultimate prize–
One's soul's software time-capsule
with all memories–saved

Log off your–by the years strained–seldom healed sight
Her inner-lit smile like a hummingbird
out of blue void appears
Put the encumbered hearing at ease and ... just stand by
His warm un-bygone laughter
ignites the twilight silence

The lost loved ones–who set sail for far off seas first
unyielding peaks conquered
by brave proudly blind youth
Its recorded intense feelings' palette and fragrance
Intact await the silver age's–now subtler–fingertips

Self-cast realities have always been covertly virtual ...
dividing rule of "then" with "now"
feeds off the fine illusion
one which–if further questioned gently and lovingly
might well fade or with Heaven's grace
even cease to exist ...

TO GO IT ALONE

To be–to still exist
Here and now
When of my wings wide
few feathers remain
From the warm sea of hope
Flow two trickles salty
Of bright lights aiming sky
A thin flame dies down
from my youth home
A chimney stands only
to live still present
Here and now
yet fly high and far
fly towards the unknown
before long…

SEMANTICS–AFTERLIFE

Hell may–perhaps–consist of inflamed dungeon
where the red and horned devils
with hairy-tails-hoofs-sharp
do their shift-work wielding the large rustic forks

But it also might be the most
tormenting and helpless dream
about own past victims the ones intended and not
now endlessly taking their best revenge
a dream one does not wake up from
–in so welcome relief
there is no waking up here
just very slowly fading from that long dream
into yet another
tangibly harsh reality

Heaven may–possibly–be grown of soft and puffy clouds
on which those choirs of androgyny-angels
blow their golden trumpets forever and ever amen

It might as well be the elated and healing dream
of meeting in joy all the closest
and loved ones who passed
about–in lightness–fulfilling own noble wishes
For in ether sculpted achievements
there is also no waking up here
but gradually fading from that fine dream
into much more tangible reality
one with it's worse just spared

These non-Dantesque sub-visions of hell and heaven
respectively look like
a lower and upper house of purgatory…

The epitome of hell–seems to be dwelling
in the unable to mature hatred
towards God hence all creation
And the actual heaven might truly mean
the utmost love devoid of self–
becoming one with its God…

THE UNEXPLAINABLE

Why is it–that always above the regular fields
with evenly grown stems of wheat
gently waving on calm wind that at night comes
there are a few spikes attracted to the moon
that oversees each half-asleep plot
slowly readying to yield its future harvest?

Their stems look the same as all the other ones
yet they appear to had sipped
some magic–flowing from within
that naturally has caused them to self-realize
through faster inching upward
somewhat further from the soil closer to faint lights

Why is it–that on the rarest land-swathes only
there fade those abandoned
made of geometric complex mandalas fragile signs
left among all the intact fields
that had not shown their magic
inviting the unexplainable for even a brief stay?

BIRD HUNTING

At evening
if the wind is right
I set my trap on a small table
A blank sheet
of paper

Wild birds–new poems
long hover above
but don't take the bait

At last
if hesitantly
the weakest of them
falls onto the paper
and dies

Others–strong and beautiful
silently soar
into darkness

LOVE STORY

A spark of love–by this world attracted
shyly submits to the healthy power of crude nature
Yet feels unfulfilled

So it searches for something
enjoys that next find
And in new pain discards the consecutive substitute

By design–longing
the further it expands beyond its five senses' walls
the closer it inches to its Aim

After outgrowing its robust bondage the mature love
begins evolving as a flame less restricted
but still–incomplete

Now it hones own readiness to accept the invitation
for dissolving itself
in the joyfully burning Endlessness

THE GIFT

Once larger-than-life tired Dyonisius was approaching the inevitable gate, now fully visible to him for the first time. It seemed so long ago when, true to his name, he drank wine, sang and danced, played the flute, or hunted deer among the green hills.

All his long and productive life he was also introducing engineering solutions, with a remarkable success of an "outside of the box" thinker. In between, he studied philosophy, explored yoga, or translated Keats. In the bygone era Dyonisius personally knew back-then important figures from the arena of politics, industry and art, made and lost fortunes.

He participated in both great wars, twice saved from imminent death by his wife. The last war took her instead. Soon their only son, an engineer like him, was killed in action. Almost nothing was left. Then he grew very old and gravely ill.

The shadows haunting him have lately become denser and darker. He helplessly watched while his body, once invincible, was quickly turning non-responsive, increasingly foreign to him. Now he genuinely yearned to depart, knowing that the time was right.

With a feeling of wise acceptance, and the nearly regained curiosity of a once unusually precise mind, the gloomy shadows started dissolving in steadily emerging light. The soothing calm did settle-in, after he re-discovered in a profound insight that nothing ever could destroy the true him—so different from his fading vehicle.

There was one remaining worry and a task

though—how to protect his only grandson, already an orphan. With no financial means, in a country ruined by war, the elder's hands were sadly empty. Yet, before the last breath, the need to do his available best for the boy became an imperative. A spike of creative clarity did come to his mind, as it used to do in the past. He opened his eyes, called the grandson, and began talking with strain.

The youngster approached his bed with a chilling thought that the only, and very last element making him not completely different from his school friends, is to be lost. He instantly knew; a year earlier his ailing mother had called him the similar way. Faced with worries about the future, he almost did not listen to the dying whispers of the old man.

Suddenly, something inside him responded, as his grandfather's pale drawn face for a brief moment became full of light. He again radiated the very familiar to the boy energy. The youngster's inner voice told him that an event beyond his hitherto experience unfolds, and that it was crucial to concentrate now.

He moved closer, to be able to look straight into the old man's eyes. Simultaneously, Dyonisius, focusing on the boy's eyes, clearly and very convincingly conveyed four short sentences: "There is much more to this world that you can see,"; "There is purpose and sense behind everything,"; "There are other worlds, and all flow from one Source,"; "You must never forget that." Then completely exhausted, he withdrew.

Dyonisius passed away before long. With no material support, no other guidance given to him by anyone, the boy went his own obstacle-ridden way, faltering but trying to learn from mistakes. Even in the worst of times, he somehow remembered those four sentences. Being brilliantly engineered, they turned to be a very long-lasting farewell gift indeed.

Predictably, the shore-less river took the youngster along. As he grew up, he became a cement factory worker, a coal miner, a stonemason, an orderly, a researcher, a psychologist, and perhaps in-a-second language writer. All his life, for some unexplained reason, he felt compelled to further and deeper explore his grandfather's farewell gift. Was that faraway boy–really me?

THREE DREAMS

for Tom Poplawski

An old man
complained to the night–
I had a dream
that the sea came
and took me away

I had a dream
that I was the day
and the sea
brought you safe ashore
replied the night

I've dreamt forever
that you all
are the dreams - of mine
The calm Sea
whispered gently…

Gallery images by Tomasz Poplawski

Zen Master, p 36

The Yoga Way, p. 37

The Old Stone House, p. 63

Hurricane Came, p. 112

Afar at the Too-Young Age, p. 104